The Dunder Mifflin

Recipe Book

Enjoy Delicious Recipes That Are Inspired
by The Office

By: Susan Gray

//

License Notices

//

Table of Contents

Introduction

Hosting a party themed after The Office? Looking for inspiration for recipes for the party? Well, look no further than this recipe book! Filled with delicious recipes that are straight from The Office, you'll have all you need right here! From Ryan's fire-starting pita to Stanley's favorite day food – Pretzels, there's everything in here for the Ultimate Office fan!

All the recipes here are detailed, simple to whip up and come with step-by-step instructions – making this book perfect for even the most beginner of cooks! So what are you waiting for? Let's get started!

1. Kevin's Chili

No recipe book based on The Office can be complete without Kevin's famous chili! Just be sure you don't spill it!

Makes: 6 servings

Prep: 10 min

Cook: 20 mins

Ingredients:

- 2 tbsp vegetable oil
- 2 cloves garlic, minced
- 1 cup chopped yellow onion
- 1 lb. lean ground beef
- ¾ cup chopped green bell pepper
- 1 tbsp chili powder
- ½ tsp paprika
- ½ tsp ground cumin
- 2 (15.25-oz) cans kidney beans, rinsed drained
- 1 tsp crushed red pepper flakes
- 1 (28-oz) can tomatoes
- 1 cup canned crushed tomatoes
- Sour cream, for serving
- Chopped green onions, for serving
- Grated cheddar cheese, for serving

Directions:

Warm the oil in a cast iron Dutch oven over medium heat on a grill or on a grate over a medium-heat fire. Add the onions cook, stirring often, for 5 minutes. Add the garlic and stir. Add the ground beef, stirring to crumble the meat while it browns. After the meat browns, add the green peppers and cook for 2 minutes more. Stir in the chili powder, paprika, cumin, kidney beans, and red pepper flakes. Add the diced tomatoes with juice and the crushed tomatoes. Stir well and simmer for 15 minutes. Serve in bowls, topped with sour cream, chopped green onions, and grated cheddar cheese.

2. Angela's Brownies

Enjoy a batch of Angela's delicious and fudgy brownies with the help of this recipe!

Makes: 16 brownies

Prep: 15 mins

Cook: 25 mins

Ingredients:

- 1 cup icing sugar
- 1 stick unsalted butter
- 3 eggs
- 1 cup all-purpose flour
- ½ cup + 2 tbsp cocoa powder
- 3 oz. dark chocolate, chopped

Directions:

Preheat the oven to 375°F. Prepare an 8x8 inch baking tin.

In a pan over low heat, combine the butter and sugar and heat until all the butter has melted.

Remove the pan from the heat. Add in the flour, eggs, and cocoa. Lastly, fold in the dark chocolate.

Pour batter into the tin. Place in the oven for about 25 mins or until the edges are set and the top looks firm.

Let the brownies cool before cutting.

3. Alfredo's Pizza

Not to be confused with the trashy Pizza by Alfredo.

Makes: 1 13 inch pizza

Prep: 1 hr. 10 mins

Cook: 20 mins

Ingredients:

For the crust:

- 2 cups all-purpose/bread flour, + more for rolling
- ½ tsp sugar
- 1 1/8 tsp (1/2 envelope) dry yeast
- 1 tsp salt
- ¾ cup water, at 110°F
- 1 tbsp + 1 tsp, olive oil

For the pizza:

- ½ cup pizza sauce, homemade or store-bought
- 30 slices pepperoni
- 1 cup cooked sausage
- 2 cups shredded mozzarella cheese
- ¼ cup parmesan cheese
- 2 tbsp fresh basil leaves
- Red pepper flakes

Directions:

In the bowl with the hook attachment, combine the yeast, flour, sugar and salt. Add the water 1 tbsp of olive oil and mix until a ball of dough is formed.

Remove and place the dough on a floured surface and knead for a few minutes into a ball.

Grease a bowl with the olive oil that remains and place it in. cover the bowl with plastic wrap and let it rise for about an hour.

Preheat the oven to 400°F.

After the dough has risen, punch it lightly to deflate. Roll it out to fit your pizza pan. Top evenly with pizza sauce, mozzarella, parmesan, sausage and pepperoni. Bake for about 15-20 mins/until the crust is golden-brown. Sprinkle on the red pepper flakes and serve!

4. Pretzels

Don't wait for the next pretzel day like Stanley! Instead, make these delicious pretzels at home, so that everyday can be pretzel day!

Makes: 8 servings

Prep: 2 hrs. 40 mins

Cook: 10 mins

Ingredients:

- 1 package active dry yeast
- 1 cup warm water
- 1 tbsp brown sugar
- 3 ¼ cups bread flour
- ½ cup cold beer
- 2 tbsp unsalted butter, cut into 1 inch pieces, at room temperature, plus more for greasing
- 2 tsp salt

Directions:

Preheat oven to 500 F.

Into a stand mixer, add in the warm water. Sprinkle on the yeast

Add in the brown sugar. Mix thoroughly and allow to bloom until foamy. This should take about 5 minutes.

Add in the flour, butter, salt, and beer, and continue stirring. On low speed, begin kneading the dough for a minute or until it forms a smooth ball. Continue kneading until the dough become pliant – about 5 minutes.

In a lightly greased bowl, place dough and cover with saran wrap. Set away to rise in a warm area for 90 minutes, until double.

Divide into 8 portions and roll out into desired shape – knots, buns, or sticks.

Arrange on 2 lined baking trays about 2 inches apart.

Allow to rise for 30 more minutes.

Coat with a quick egg wash before baking for 8-10 minutes until crispy and golden brown!

5. Osso Buco

Just like the Osso Bucco in Jan's disastrous dinner party!

Makes: 6 servings

Prep: 5 mins

Cook: 2 hrs.

Ingredients:

- 1-1/2 cups sliced mushrooms
- 1 1.2 cups chopped onions
- 2 tbsp coconut oil
- 1 cup beef stock
- 1/2 tsp salt
- 1/4 tsp ground black pepper
- 1 tsp minced garlic
- 1 tsp chopped parsley
- 4 pounds osso buco

Directions:

Put all recipe ingredients in a casserole dish, cover and bake for 2 hours on 400F. Onions and mushrooms should be almost melted and turned into a sauce after 2 hours.

Garnish with chopped parsley and serve.

6. Meatballs

Just like the classic prank that Dwight and Stanley pull off on Jim, you'll have tons of meatballs for dinner.

Makes: 8 servings

Prep: 10 mins

Cook: 8 hrs.

Ingredients:

- 1 1/2 pounds lean ground beef
- 1 cup uncooked long-grain white rice
- 1 small yellow onion, peeled finely chopped
- 3 cloves garlic, minced
- 2 tsp dried parsley
- 1/2 tbsp dried dill
- 1 large egg
- 1/4 cup all-purpose flour
- 2 cups tomato juice or tomato-vegetable juice
- 2–4 cups water
- 2 tbsp butter
- Salt to taste
- Freshly ground black pepper to taste

Directions:

Make meatballs by mixing together the ground beef with the rice, onion, garlic, parsley, dill, egg in a bowl; shape into meatballs roll each one in flour.

Add the tomato/tomato-vegetable juice to a 4-quart slow cooker. Add in the meatballs. Pour water to completely cover the meatballs. Add in the butter.

Cover cook on low 6–8 hours, checking periodically to make sure the cooker doesn't boil dry. Add salt and pepper to taste.

7. Fettuccini Alfredo

Carbo-load on this fettuccini Alfredo pasta before your big marathon race.

Makes: 6 servings

Prep: 20 mins

Cook: 25 mins

Ingredients:

Homemade Noodles:

- 3 cups all-purpose flour
- Salt
- 3 eggs
- 3 tbsp lukewarm water

Alfredo Sauce:

- 2/3 cup heavy cream
- 1/2 cup butter or margarine
- 1 1/4 cups grated Parmesan cheese
- 1/4 tsp salt
- 1/8 tsp pepper
- Parsley, chopped

Directions:

Homemade Noodles: In medium bowl, combine flour and 1/2 tsp salt. Make well in center. Add eggs and water; beat vigorously with fork until ingredients are well combined. Dough will be stiff. Put on floured surface, knead until smooth elastic, about 15 minutes. Cover with a bowl; let rest 10 minutes.

Divide dough into 4 parts. Keep covered with bowl until ready to roll out. Roll out each part to paper thinness, a 12-inch square. Sprinkle lightly with flour. Then roll loosely around rolling pin, as for jelly roll. Slip out rolling pin. With sharp knife, cut into 1/8-inch wide strips for fine noodles, 1/3-inch wide strips for broad noodles. Arrange strips on an ungreased cookie pan.

In a kettle, bring four quarts water with 1 tbsp salt to boiling. Add noodles; return to boiling. Boil, uncovered, until tender, about 20-25 mins. Drain noodles; keep warm.

Alfredo Sauce: Heat cream and butter in medium saucepan until butter or margarine is melted. Remove from heat. Stir in 1 cup Parmesan cheese, salt and pepper until sauce is well-blended and fairly smooth. Add to noodles; toss until well coated. Sprinkle with chopped parsley remaining Parmesan cheese. Serve at once.

8. Bacon

Please don't grill your foot on your George Foreman. Instead, try this easy (and safe) recipe for delicious grilled bacon.

Makes: 4 servings

Prep: 5 mins

Cook: 20-30 mins

Ingredients:

- 1 tbsp salted butter
- 1 pound thick-cut bacon

Directions:

In the skillet over med. heat, melt the butter.

Add each piece of bacon to the skillet. Do not overcrowd the skillet. Fry the bacon for 4-5 mins. per side until crisp. Transfer to a wire rack to drain. Repeat until all the bacon is cooked.

9. Potato Salad

No, you don't have to pick up potato salad from the supermarket like Michael. Instead, you can easily make it at home with the help of this recipe!

Makes: 6 servings

Prep: 1 hr.

Cook: 10 mins

Ingredients:

- 2 pounds Yukon Gold potatoes, cleaned cut into quarters
- ½ sweet onion, thinly sliced and then chopped
- 4 hard-boiled eggs, peeled
- 1 cup mayonnaise, plus more as needed
- 1 tsp Colman's dry mustard
- Salt and freshly ground black pepper

Directions:

Place the potatoes in a deep stockpot, cover with water, and boil until tender. Drain and let cool to room temperature. Peel the potatoes cut into bite-size pieces. Place in a medium bowl. Sprinkle the chopped onions over the top, cover with plastic wrap, and refrigerate until well chilled.

When ready to serve, cut up the eggs and add to the potatoes. Add the mayonnaise mustard and mix well. Season to taste with salt and pepper. Serve.

10. Lasagna

Hopefully, this lasagna won't have too much power over you like it does on warehouse Madge.

Makes: 8 servings

Prep: 25 mins

Cook: 1 ½ hrs.

Ingredients:

- Unsalted butter, for the dish
- 1 recipe (4 cups) Thick Béchamel
- ½ recipe (6 sheets; about 8 ounces) Fresh Pasta Sheet
- ½ recipe (3 cups) Ragu Bolognese, warm
- 4 oz. freshly grated Parmesan cheese

Directions:

Preheat oven to 375F.

Assemble the lasagna: Mix together ½ cup of the béchamel sauce and ¼ cup of room-temperature water spread it in a 9 x 13-inch (3-quart) glass or ceramic baking dish, then top with one third of the noodles (2 sheets). Spread one cup of the béchamel sauce on the pasta and cover with 1½ cups of the Bolognese sauce. Sprinkle with ⅓ cup of the Parmesan. Repeat with another layer of noodles, 1 cup of the béchamel, the remaining Bolognese sauce, and ⅓ cup of the Parmesan. Top with the remaining noodles, béchamel, and Parmesan.

Bake the lasagna: Cover with foil and bake for 30 mins. Uncover bake until bubbling and the top is golden, about 20 minutes longer. Let rest for 15 minutes before cutting into squares and serving.

11. Lemonade

Don't forget to put a ñ on top!

Makes: 12 servings

Prep: 10 mins

Cook: -

Ingredients:

- 4 cups cold water
- 3 lemons, washed and deseeded
- Juice of 1 large lemon
- ¾ cup sugar

Directions:

Blend all ingredients shown above on high speed in a high-quality blender. Strain before serving.

12. Michael's French Toast

Make this delicious French toast when starting your own paper company.

Makes: 4 servings

Prep: 5 mins

Cook: 10 mins

Ingredients:

- 4 eggs
- 1 ½ cups milk
- ½ cup white sugar
- 2 loaves challah bread, sliced
- Unsalted butter

Directions:

Heat a skillet over med heat generously grease with butter.

Combine the milk, sugar and eggs in a large bowl. Put the slices of bread into the mixture until well coated on both sides.

Place the bread slices into the skillet and cook for 1-2 minutes on each side or until crisp and brown. Repeat as many times as needed.

Serve with your favorite toppings.

13. Tiramisu

You don't need to fish tiramisu out of the bin to enjoy it!
Just follow this super easy recipe instead!

Makes: 4-6 servings

Prep: 4 hrs.

Cook: -

Ingredients:

- 2 egg yolks
- 2 tbsp caster sugar
- 1 cup mascarpone or cream cheese
- ½ cup ml strong black coffee
- Drops of vanilla essence
- 2 cups sponge fingers
- Cocoa powder

Directions:

In a bowl, beat up the yolks sugar together till the mixture becomes pale and creamy.

Add the vanilla essence fold in the mascarpone.

Make strong black coffee. Put the sponge fingers in the coffee, just enough so that they can absorb the liquid. Any longer and they will crumble and fall apart.

Arrange a layer of sponge fingers in a dish cover them with the mascarpone. Continue making layers of sponge fingers, followed by mascarpone, ensuring that the topmost layer is of mascarpone.

Put the tiramisu in the refrigerator for three–four hours, dust on top with cocoa powder serve.

14. Michael's Birthday Donuts

Celebrate Michael's birthday with these delicious donuts!

Makes: 6 servings

Prep: 10 mins

Cook: 8 mins

Ingredients:

For the donuts:

- 1/8 tsp salt
- ½ cup all-purpose flour
- ¼ cup white sugar
- ¼ tsp baking soda
- 1 small egg or ½ a large egg
- ¼ tsp vanilla extract
- 2 tbsp milk
- 3 tbsp sour cream
- 2 tbsp vegetable oil

For the glaze:

- 1 tbsp milk
- ¾ cup icing sugar
- ½ tsp vanilla extract

Directions:

For the donuts:

Preheat the oven to 375°F. Then grease a donut pan and set aside.

In a medium-size bowl, mix the salt, sugar, baking soda, and flour.

In a small bowl, beat together the remaining ingredients. Add it to the flour mixture and beat again until just combined.

Spoon mixture into the pan and bake for 8 minutes. Set aside to cool.

For glaze:

In a bowl, mix together the vanilla, milk and icing sugar. Dip the cooled donuts in the glaze to coat and place on a wire rack to set. Serve.

15. Tacos

Hopefully you can enjoy these tacos a bit more than Nellie did!

Makes: 6 servings

Prep: 5 mins

Cook: 10 mins

Ingredients:

- ½ tsp shortening
- 2 tbsp green onion, chopped
- ½ can taco sauce
- ½ cup grated cheddar cheese
- ½ package taco shells
- ½ cup cooked chicken, shredded
- Salt to taste
- 4 oz. green chili salsa

Directions:

Cook the onions in a bit of oil for 2 mins. Add in the chicken and salsa and bring to boil. Set aside.

Cook the tacos according to the box instructions. Divide the chicken mixture equally among the tacos and then top with cheese. Serve with lettuce, tomato and guacamole.

16. Jim's Ham and Cheese Sandwich

Recipe for Jim's daily ham and cheese sandwich!

Makes: 2 sandwiches

Prep: 5 mins

Cook: 5 mins

Ingredients:

- 4 slices white bread
- Butter
- 4 slices ham
- Mustard
- 8 Swiss cheese slice

Directions:

Heat skillet and brush with butter. Spread some butter on 1 side of bread slice. Put it butter-side-down on a plate. Add a thin layer of mustard onto the other slice. Put a cheese slice on the first slice followed by a slice of ham followed by another cheese slice. Top with the mustard slice. Brush outside with more butter. Repeat with other slices.

Place on the skillet and cook for golden brown.

Serve.

17. Baklava

All Stanley likes is baklava now. And with this recipe, we can see why.

Makes: 30 pieces

Prep: 45 mins

Cook: 40 mins

Ingredients:

- 3½ cups finely chopped mixed nuts, such as walnuts, almonds, and/or pistachio nuts
- 1½ sticks (12 tbsp) butter, plus ½ tsp for greasing
- 14 sheets of phyllo pastry
- 2 tbsp sugar
- 1 tsp ground cinnamon

Syrup

- 1⅔ cups sugar
- 1¼ cups water
- 1 tbsp lemon juice
- 3 tbsp honey
- 2 small cinnamon sticks

Directions:

Preheat the oven to 350°F. Line a baking sheet with parchment paper. Spread out the nuts on the prepared sheet and bake in the oven for 5–10 minutes. Do not turn off the oven.

Melt the butter in a saucepan. Grease a 10 x 14-inch baking pan with some of the melted butter and place one sheet of phyllo on top. Brush the phyllo with more melted butter. Continue layering the phyllo and brushing with melted butter until there are five layers of phyllo in the pan.

Mix the nuts with the sugar and ground cinnamon. Sprinkle one-third of the mixture over the phyllo, then cover with two more buttered layers of phyllo. Sprinkle half the remaining nut mixture over the phyllo and cover with two more layers of buttered phyllo. Sprinkle the nut mix over the pastry, cover with five layers of buttered phyllo, fold in all the overhanging edges. Cut the baklava, then bake for 25–30 mins.

Meanwhile, make the syrup. Put the sugar water into a saucepan, stir and place over low heat until the sugar has dissolved. Increase the heat to med, bring to a boil, then add the lemon juice, honey, and cinnamon sticks. Reduce the heat simmer for 10 mins. Remove from the heat and let cool.

Pour the syrup over the baklava and let stand until the phyllo has absorbed all the syrup. The flavor of the baklava will mature for one or two days.

18. Fennel Arugula Salad

A delicious salad that even Angela would approve of.

Makes: 4 servings

Prep: 10 mins

Cook: -

Ingredients:

For the salad:

- 1 fennel bulb, thinly sliced
- 2 cups packed arugula
- 2 medium apples, thinly sliced
- 1 medium zucchini, shredded (about 1 cup)
- 1/4 cup chopped fresh mint (optional)

For the dressing:

- 3 tbsp olive oil
- 1 tbsp honey
- Juice of 1/2 lemon
- 1 tsp grated lemon zest
- 1 clove garlic, minced
- 1/4 tsp sea salt
- 1/4 tsp freshly ground black pepper

Directions:

For salad: In a bowl, combine together the fennel, apple, arugula, zucchini, and mint if using.

For dressing: In a bowl, combine together the olive oil, honey, lemon juice, lemon zest, garlic, salt, pepper.

Toss and serve.

19. Pita

Just don't start a fire like Ryan when you're making this recipe.

Makes: 6-10 servings

Prep: 1 hr. 20 mins

Cook: 10 mins

Ingredients:

- 3 cups whole wheat flour
- 1 cup warm water
- 1 1/2 tsp yeast
- 2 tbsp honey
- 1 tbsp oil

Directions:

Combine yeast and water. Let sit 10 minutes to activate yeast.

Combine oil, honey and yeast mixture.

Slowly add flour to yeast mixture.

Let rise for one hour.

Divide dough into eight equal parts. Knead each part for one minute.

Roll dough flat. Cut into a seven inch circle. Put circles on baking stone. Let rise for one hour.

Preheat oven to 450 degrees. Bake for 7 minutes. Serve!

20. Chicken Pot Pie

Snooze off like Michael when you eat this delicious chicken pot pie.

Makes: 4 servings

Prep: 45 mins

Cook: 1 hr.

Ingredients:

For the Chicken Filling

- 1 tbsp olive oil

- 2 boneless, skinless chicken breasts

- 2 tbsp salted butter, divided

- 5 large carrots, diced

- 1 Vidalia or other sweet onion, minced

- 2 garlic cloves, minced

- 1 cup cremini mushrooms, cleaned and sliced

- 2½ cups whole milk

- ½ cup heavy (whipping) cream

- 2 cups butter beans

- ½ tsp ground chipotle chile pepper

- Sea salt

- Freshly ground black pepper

- 1 tsp baking powder

- 2 tbsp all-purpose flour

For the Biscuit Topping

- 2 cups all-purpose flour
- 1 tsp baking soda
- 1 tsp sea salt
- ½ cup (1 stick) cold salted butter, cubed
- 1 cup buttermilk

To Make the Chicken Filling

Directions:

In a skillet over medium heat, heat the oil and cook the chicken for 5 to 6 minutes per side. Remove, chop, and set aside.

Return the skillet to medium heat. Add 1 tbsp of butter and the carrots. Sauté for 3 to 5 minutes.

Add the onion and garlic to the skillet. Cook for 5 mins, until the onion begins to brown.

Add the mushrooms. Cook for 4 to 6 minutes, stirring frequently, until they soften.

In a med saucepan over med-high heat, scald the milk and cream by bringing it almost to a boil then remove. Set aside.

Add the butter beans to the skillet, along with the chicken and chipotle chile pepper. Season with sea salt and black pepper. Cook for 2-3 mins, stirring frequently.

Add the flour and 1 tbsp of scalded milk to the skillet. Stir well to incorporate. Continue stirring and slowly pour in the remaining milk.

Preheat the oven to 350°F.

To Make the Biscuit Topping

In a med bowl, mix the flour, baking soda, baking powder, sea salt.

Add the cold butter cubes in mix together with your hands, crumbling the butter, until the texture resembles coarse cornmeal.

Stir in the buttermilk.

Put the dough out onto a floured work surface (or a silicone baking mat) and pat it out flat into a 12-by-16-inch rectangle about one inch thick, sprinkling with a bit of flour to keep the dough from sticking. Fold in half and repeat 3 times. With a biscuit cutter, cut out 10 biscuits. Arrange the biscuits on top of the potpie filling.

Bake for 30-35 mins, until the biscuits rise and are cooked through, and the filling is bubbling.

21. Meatball Subs

Don't worry! Unlike in The Office, this meatball parm sub is actually delicious!

Makes: 8 servings

Prep: 10 mins

Cook: 20 mins

Ingredients:

- 1 cup celery, diced
- 1 cup carrots, diced
- 1 cup onion, diced
- 5 cloves garlic, minced
- 1 ½ cups fresh parsley, chopped
- 1 ½ cup breadcrumbs
- 1 cup parmesan cheese, divided
- 2 large eggs
- 4 tbsp ketchup
- Salt and pepper
- 3 lb. ground beef
- 8 sandwich rolls, halved lengthwise and toasted
- 2 cups marinara sauce
- 2 cups shredded mozzarella cheese

Directions:

Preheat the oven to 400°F. Line a baking pan with baking paper and set aside.

In a large bowl, combine the diced vegetables, garlic, fresh parsley, breadcrumbs, ½ cup parmesan cheese, eggs and ketchup. Season with salt and pepper. Add the beef and mix again until just combined.

Form 1 ½ inch meatballs and place on the baking sheet. Bake for about 20 mins or until meatballs are browned.

In the meantime, heat the marinara sauce in a saucepan until warm. Spoon marinara evenly over the meatballs and top with shredded mozzarella. Place the pan back in the oven for about 3 minutes or until the cheese has melted.

Place the meatballs in the toasted rolls and sprinkle evenly with the remaining parmesan cheese.

Serve.

22. Detox Juice

Perfect for your office's weight loss program! Just don't overdo it like Kelly.

Makes: 4 cups

Prep: 3 mins

Cook: 25 mins plus chilling time

Ingredients:

- 4 cups water
- 2 green tea bags
- 1 tbsp lemon juice
- 4 (½-inch) slices fresh ginger
- 2 tsp honey

Directions:

Bring the water ginger to boil in a pan, then lower, cover, simmer for ten mins. Remove add in the tea bags, steep for 10 minutes.

Remove the tea bags ginger, and then stir in the lemon juice and honey. Chill for 1 hr. before serving over ice.

23. Mini Chocolate Cupcakes

Even though Kevin doesn't agree with them, mini cupcakes are delicious and this recipe is here to prove it!

Makes: 24 mini cupcakes

Prep: 25 mins

Cook: 20 mins

Ingredients:

For the cupcakes:

- 3/4 tsp baking powder
- 3/4 cup all-purpose flour
- 1/2 cup dark cocoa powder
- 1 tsp espresso powder
- 1/2 tsp baking soda
- 1/2 cup white sugar
- 1/2 cup light brown sugar
- 1/3 cup vegetable oil
- 2 tsp vanilla extract
- 2 large eggs
- 1/4 tsp salt
- 1/2 cup buttermilk

For the frosting:

- 5 oz. dark chocolate chips
- 5 oz. milk chocolate chips
- 10 oz. heavy cream
- Chocolate shavings, for decoration

Directions:

For the cupcakes:

Preheat the oven to 350F. Prepare a mini cupcake pan with 24 liners.

In a bowl, whisk the dry ingredients together and set aside.

In a bowl, whisk the sugars, eggs, oil vanilla until well combined and smooth. Add in 1/2 of the dry ingredients and then half of the buttermilk and whisk until just combined. Repeat with remaining dry mixture and buttermilk and stir until just combined.

Gently pour in the batter into cupcake liners and bake for 18-22 mins.

Set aside cupcakes to cool.

For the frosting:

In a large bowl, combine dark and milk chocolate chips.

In a medium-sized bowl, place cream and heat in the microwave until cream just starts to boil. Pour cream on the chocolate chips and let stand for 2 minutes.

Gently start whisking the mixture until smooth. Place in the refrigerator for about 1 or so.

Using a hand mixer, whip the ganache for 3-4 minutes until light and fluffy.

24. Vanilla Ice Cream

Like Andy found out the hard way, ice cream is not to be shared!

Makes: 6 servings

Prep: 3 hrs.

Cook: 10 mins

Ingredients:

- 2 cups whipping cream
- 4 egg yolks
- Pinch of salt
- 2 tsp vanilla extract
- 2 cups half and half
- 2 cups milk
- 1 cup white sugar

Directions:

Put a saucepan over medium-high heat and in that saucepan, mix together 2 cups of milk, pinch of salt, sugar and the 4 egg yolks. Stir the mixture until it starts to simmer. Lower the heat and whisk for a further 5 minutes or until the mixture thickens.

Then add in 2 cups of half and half, 2 cups of cream and the vanilla extract. Wisk until combined. Put the prepared mixture in an airtight container and pop it in the fridge for about 3 hours.

Churn in an ice cream maker.

25. Pesto

Just like Ryan's mom's pesto!

Makes: 6 servings

Prep: 10 mins

Cook: -

Ingredients:

- 1/4 cup pine nuts or walnuts
- 1/3 cup olive oil
- 1 cup fresh basil
- 2 cloves garlic, peeled
- 1/4 cup Parmesan cheese, grated
- 1/4 tsp salt
- 1/4 cup fresh parsley
- 1/8 tsp pepper

Directions:

In a blender or food processor, chop nuts and garlic. Add half of the olive oil, basil and parsley and blend. Add remaining half and blend until smooth. Slowly add cheese, salt and pepper and blend until smooth. The finished sauce should be slightly runny.

26. Samosa

Perfect recipe for when you're hosting a Diwali party!

Makes: 10 servings

Prep: 20 mins

Cook: 10 mins

Ingredients:

Samosa Dough –

- 2 ½ cup all-purpose flour
- 1 tsp ajwain (carom seed)
- 1 tsp salt
- 4 tbsp ghee or oil
- Water

Filling –

- 2 tbsp ghee or oil
- 1 tsp cumin
- 1 inch ginger, chopped
- 4-5 potatoes, boiled and mashed
- ½ tsp mango powder
- 1 tsp red chili powder
- 1 tsp cilantro powder
- 1 tsp garam masala

Pomegranate mixture -

- 1 tbsp cilantro powder
- 1 tsp dried pomegranate

Directions:

For dough, mix all the ingredients for it together and just enough water to create a tough dough. Cover and set aside.

For filling, heat the ghee in a pan. Add in the rest of the ingredients and cook until combined.

In a separate small pan, roast the 1 tbsp of cilantro powder and 1 tsp of pomegranate seeds. Once roasted, crush into a rough paste.

Add this paste to the potato mixture and combine thoroughly.

To make the samosas, divide the dough into 10 pieces.

Roll each piece into a circle of 1/8 inch thickness and cut it into half, giving you 2 semi circles.

Place a bowl of a little water next to you and move onto the next step.

Hold one corner of the semi-circle and rolling the dough into a cone shape, overlap with the other corner, sticking them together with some water.

Fill the cone with the potato mixture, making sure to leave about ¼ - ½ inch of dough on top. Press the top of the cone together with some water to finish making the samosa.

Do this with the rest of the dough and potato mixture.

Heat oil on low.

Fry the samosas on low for about 8-10 minutes until crisp and brown.

Serve with your favorite sauces or condiments and enjoy!

27. Tuna Sandwich

Eat this sandwich once and be called Big Tuna by Andy for the rest of your life.

Makes: 3 servings

Prep: 10 mins

Cook: -

Ingredients:

- 2 cans tuna in water
- ½ cup mayonnaise
- 1 tbsp minced red onion
- ½ tbsp lemon juice
- 1 small garlic clove, minced
- 1 tbsp pickle relish
- 6 sliced bread

Directions:

Combine all of the above ingredients till pickle relish. Put on 3 slices of bread and top with another the remaining 3 slices.

Serve.

28. Office Birthday Cake

Be prepared for the next office birthday with this delicious cake recipe!

Makes: 6 servings

Prep: 15 mins

Cook: 20 mins

Ingredients:

For cake:

- ¾ tsp baking soda
- 1 cup all-purpose flour
- 1 cup white sugar
- ½ tsp salt
- 1 tsp baking powder
- 2 tsp espresso powder, divided
- ½ cup milk buttermilk
- 4 tbsp vegetable oil
- 6 tbsp unsweetened cocoa powder
- 1 large egg
- 1 tsp vanilla extract
- ½ cup hot water

For the ganache frosting:

- 6 oz. semi-sweet chocolate chips
- 6 oz. heavy cream

Directions:

Preheat the oven to 350°F. Line two 6" cake pans with baking paper and grease lightly.

In a medium-sized bowl, combine the dry ingredients set aside.

In a bowl, beat together the buttermilk, oil, egg and vanilla extract for 1 minute. Add in the dry mixture whisk until well combined.

Combine the hot water with 1 ½ tsp espresso powder. Stream it into the cake batter carefully and whisk again until well combined.

Divide batter evenly between the cake pans and bake for 20 minutes.

For the Frosting:

Place chocolate chips in a large bowl.

Heat the cream in a saucepan/microwave until it just starts to boil. Pour over the chocolate chips and let stand for 2 minutes. Gently whisk until the mixture is smooth.

Place in the refrigerator for about 1 hr.

After an hour, use a hand mixer and whip the ganache for about 4 minutes or until light and fluffy.

Frost the cooled cake, serve and enjoy!

29. Beet Root Pie

Bears. Beets. Battestar Galactica. This delicious beet root pie is one Dwight would approve of.

Makes: 12 slices

Prep: 30 mins

Cook: 2 hrs.

Ingredients:

- 8 filo pastry sheets, pre-packaged
- 5 beet roots, diced
- 5 eggs, large
- 1 3/4 oz. of basil, chopped
- 1 3/4 oz. of parsley, chopped
- 3 1/2 oz. of Feta cheese, crumbled
- 3 1/2 oz. of spinach, chopped
- 1 onion, grated
- 1 tsp of pepper, ground
- Oil, olive
- 7 1/2 fluid oz. of water, filtered

Directions:

Wash beet root and trim stalks down. Place in saucepan. Cover it with filtered water. Bring to boil till it softens. This usually takes 35-40 minutes.

After beet root has cooked, drain and allow to cool for 1/2 hour. Wear gloves to rub beet root skin gently away. Dice into chunks. Place in large sized bowl.

To create the filling, add onion, ground pepper, cheese, spinach, basil, parsley and eggs to beet root. Mix well.

Layer the sheets of pre-made filo pastry atop each other. Brush olive oil between them as you're laying them down. Once six of the eight sheets have been laid, add beet root filling over the top.

Repeat layering till you have six of eight sheets atop filling. Each should be brushed with olive oil. Brush on thin oil layer over top.

Bake in 350F oven for an hour, or till they are a golden brown in color. Remove.

Pour 1/2 cup filtered water over top. Pour 1/2 cup water around edges. Cover with two small tea towels. Allow to set for an hour. Serve.

30. New York Sushi

Authentic New-York style sushi that you don't have to go to Tokyo for.

Makes: 6 pieces

Prep: 25 mins

Cook: -

Ingredients:

- 1 ½ cups cooked Sushi Rice
- 4 oz., sashimi grade, thinly sliced lengthwise Fresh Eel ()
- 4oz, diced Cucumber
- 4oz, thinly sliced Avocado
- 2oz. Caviar
- 1/2 tsp Sesame Oil
- 1 sheet, halved Nori
- 2 tbsp Sesame Seeds
- Special Equipment/Tools Needed:
- Bamboo Mat
- Plastic Wrap (to cover bamboo mat)
- Tezu (mixture4 of 2 tsp rice vinegar and ¼ cup water)

Directions:

Combine eel, cucumber, and sesame oil in a medium bowl.

Cover your bamboo mat with plastic wrap; then lay it on a flat surface.

Layer your avocado slices on the bottom edge of the mat.

Place your nori on your mat, starting on top of the salmon slice with the silkier side facing down.

Top with ¾ cup of your Sushi rice. Carefully wet your fingertips in tezu then proceed to spread the rice evenly over the nori. Once spread evenly sprinkle with sesame seeds.

Gently flip your sheet of nori over so that the rice is left flat on the salmon and bamboo mat.

Line up the edge of your nori sheet and avocado with the bamboo mat then spread your eel mixture at the bottom end of the nori, then top your filling with drippings of caviar.

Placing your index and middle fingers in front of your filling, position your thumbs below the bamboo mat and roll the mat over to form a tight cylinder.

Begin to roll the mat into tight cylindrical shapes keeping a gentle pressure on the mat. Roll until at the end.

When you have reached the end of your nori sheet, release the mat and lift the Sushi roll off the mat gently.

Using a clean, sharp knife, cut the roll into 6 equal pieces. Clean your knife after each slice.

Remove plastic wrap and Enjoy!

Conclusion

Well, there you have it! 30 delicious recipes inspired by The Office! Hope you've enjoyed all these recipes and make sure you share these recipes with your fellow Office fans and also your friends and family!

About the Author

Susan Gray is a restaurateur and writer born in Maui, Hawaii, and spent the first 18 years of her life there. Her first step in cooking was influenced by her mother who managed a catering company and involved her in lots of her cooking. That experience was the eye-opener for her.

When she left home for college, she worked briefly in the kitchen of a restaurant close to her college, where she was studying to have a degree in nutrition and dietetics at The Steinhardt School of Culture, Education, and Human Development. Her experiences at the restaurant, coupled with her degree laid the map before her.

She stayed in New York after her degree, where she met her husband. Together, they started their restaurant business, and it hit the roof. Susan, however, felt that there was more to do. She figured that she could help people discover and unlock the many tastes and experiences associated with cooking. She decided to write as much as she can to help people get the best out of their diet through food.

She has since been writing and publishing categories of recipes in a host of online and offline publications. And she is having absolute fun doing so.

//

Author's Afterthoughts

In the beginning, I wasn't quite sure if I should take the plunge and write this book. But I thought that there might be people out there who are looking for this sort of thing, and I would be failing them if I don't get down and get this thing out. See? You, my dear reader, made me do this. That's how much power you have.

I'm excited and humbled that you went for this book out of all the options available. It's nothing short of gratifying.

I would like to hear back from you. What do you think about this book? Please leave your comments as a review on Amazon. It would mean a whole lot to me.

Thank you for being so awesome.

Susan Gray

Made in the USA
Columbia, SC
20 December 2020

29493609R00057